The Classic Mantle

The Classic
MANTLE

Text by Buzz Bissinger

Photographs by Marvin E. Newman

STEWART, TABORI & CHANG | NEW YORK

I remember the year, 1962, when I was seven years old. I know it was a Sunday in May when doubleheaders were still commonplace. I know it was my first game ever at Yankee Stadium, for me far more important than a pilgrimage to the Vatican to talk baseball with the pope. I know I was with my father. I know the opponents were the hapless Washington Senators, which meant he probably got the tickets for free. I know the seats were many rows up on the mezzanine level, leaving any ball hit to the last third of the outfield up to the imagination.

It did not matter.

In the second game that day, an easy win in which Jim Bouton pitched a complete game shutout despite giving up seven hits and seven walks, Mickey Mantle hit two home runs. I won't say I remember the trajectory of the ball, but memory isn't for literal remembrance anyway, so the arc of the ball in each instance was high and explosive, neither one a little squeaker just clearing the fence. Because in the mind of a child, the Mick never hit squeakers anyway. And most of the time he didn't.

It seemed to me on that day of May in 1962 that everything

Batting left-handed, Yankee
Stadium, 1955

PREVIOUS: On deck waiting to hit at
Yankee Stadium, 1954

about Mantle was right, the essence of what a great baseball player should be and represent. I loved the way he looked in the on-deck circle, on one knee in rapt attention, eyes lasered on the pitcher to see what he was throwing. Like everyone else, I noticed the way he ran the bases after he hit those home runs, with his head ducked down so as not to show anyone up, but also, as if it were possible, to try not to draw attention to himself.

I knew the Mantle lore, as any baseball kid from New York did—the "tape measure" home run against the Senators in April 1953 that left Griffith Stadium in the nation's capital and was pegged at 565 feet before it landed in a backyard; the shot in 1956, once again off the Senators, this time at Yankee Stadium, that came within eighteen inches of leaving the Stadium before it caromed off the upper-deck facade and would have traveled an estimated 600 feet had the flight been unimpeded; the shot in 1963 off Kansas City A's pitcher Bill Fischer at the Stadium that once again would have been the first fair ball ever hit out of Yankee Stadium were it not for the gap of several feet to the top facade; the twelve World Series he appeared in, seven of them won by the Yankees, in which he hit 18 home runs and drove in 40 runs, both major league records; the more pedestrian dingers that routinely cleared 400 feet.

I knew he was fast, not as fast as he was at the beginning of his major league career, in 1951, when nobody had seen anyone run that fast to first base, but still in my mind fast enough. I longed to have been old enough to appreciate his greatest season ever, 1956,

Batting left-handed, Yankee Stadium, 1955

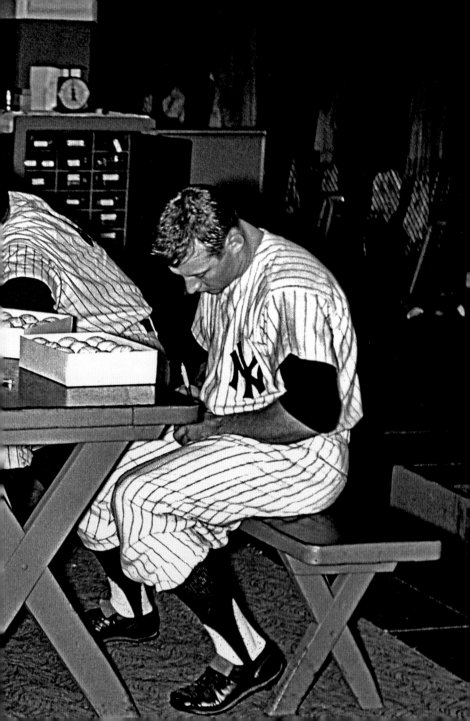

when he won the Triple Crown. I had followed the epic home run derby between him and Roger Maris in 1961 in which it had been assumed that Mickey would be the one to topple the Babe's mark of 60 had he not gotten hurt.

I was not aware of his legendary carousing in the 1950s with partners in crime Billy Martin and Whitey Ford and Hank Bauer. I knew nothing of his drinking. I knew nothing of his self-hatred, a man who despite all his accomplishments was as hard and relentless on himself as any man has ever been. I knew nothing of the pathos and bathos of his descent after his playing days were over and he might as well have been an unmoored buoy in an untamed sea.

But no child in the Mantle era had knowledge of any of that. In my very first game at the Stadium he did exactly what I hoped he would do, what all of us who watched him hoped he would do at any given moment.

Be epic.

Mickey Mantle has been dead for seventeen years. Given his career and life, it seems impossible that he has been gone that long. He still resonates in the public awareness, has a front-of-the-line place, unforgotten like virtually all other sports figures are inevitably forgotten. You can still see the all-American blond hair and shy smile of a boy from Oklahoma who conquered not only the greatest city in the world but also the world's toughest collective critics in which his mission, even if he chose not to accept it, was

PREVIOUS: Clockwise from left: Ford (16), Rizzuto, Noren, Berra, unknown player, and Mantle, 1953

At bat in a toy ball game, Yankee Stadium locker room, 1955

somehow to replace the great DiMaggio in his mansion of center field in the early 1950s. You can still see the gaunt frame withering into death as the cancer ate through him, when the smile, no longer boyish, had the poignancy of tragedy and regret but also dignity.

And, of course, you can still see the number 7 etched into the blue pinstripes of his uniform like the brightest star, a talisman of the supernatural. You can still see the monstrous back-to-front swing, where nothing was ever left out. And you can still see those home runs like the instant formation of the biggest rainbow, flying into the sky to shove aside the Big Dipper. The Natural? The comparison has been made a million times. But he was the Natural in every way possible, on the field and off of it.

Certainly Mantle's play in the caverns of old Yankee Stadium did make him unique, more than unique, right up there with DiMaggio and the great ghosts of Ruth and Gehrig when he was anywhere close to healthy, which he never really was, going back to his days as a teenager. He deserves his place among the center-field monuments. He always played hard despite constant and unimaginable pain in his legs. He even played well when he was miserably hungover, mustered by his cantankerous manager, Casey Stengel, to pinch-hit in the seventh of one game, even though the vapors of alcohol carried to Queens, and still able to hit a home run. He was a switch-hitter thanks to his father, Mutt, who started to teach him how to bat from both sides of the plate when he was four. There

Batting left-handed, Yankee Stadium, 1955

FOLLOWING: Batting right- and left-handed at Yankee Stadium, 1954

was the incomprehensible speed in addition to the incomprehensible power despite chronic osteomyelitis, a bone infection in his left ankle stemming from being kicked above the shin in a high school football game.

Even with the wreckage of his right knee that took place in the 1951 World Series, in his first major league season, he still could have hit close to 1.000 by doing nothing but drag bunting from the left side and racing to the bag. Perhaps the most remarkable feat against the Senators in 1953, when he hit at that time the longest home run ever recorded, is how later in the game he drag-bunted the ball all the way to second base and still beat the throw for a single, prompting the *New York Times* to wonder if in the course of one game, he had hit both the longest home run ever and the longest successful bunt ever.

Mantle played eighteen years for the Yankees. He extended that career four years too long because of those multiple injuries and the wrenching sight of him mummifying his legs in tape from ankle to thigh before he walked onto the field. But his statistics were still legendary: 2,401 games, 536 home runs, 1,509 runs batted in, 1,733 walks, an OPS of .977, a batting average of .298.

Great stats. One of only seven players at the time to be elected to the Baseball Hall of Fame in his first year of eligibility. But other players have had great stats. Ted Williams, who routinely fought it out with Mantle for Most Valuable Player during the 1950s, finished with a career average of .344 and 521 home runs and 1,839 runs batted in during nineteen seasons, not to mention 2,021

Bandaging his legs before the game,
in the Yankee Stadium locker room

walks and an OPS of 1.116. Williams also was a grand character, rough and gruff and blunt and a true artist of hitting. But he still wasn't Mickey Mantle.

Most athletes keep their lives under lock and key, fanatically protective of their personalities perhaps because so many, particularly in today's era, don't want fans to discover they actually don't have one. Because of the process of sports, a highly tuned assembly line in which the potentially great ones are identified in elementary school and still in single digits, they become coveted and spoiled and inward.

What distinguished Mantle was a total willingness to be human, a profound openness in which he ultimately decided there could be no secrets in his life regardless of how horrible they were. As my college roommate Harry O'Mealia put it, a great baseball fan and the most literate man I know, so many millions saw a reflection of themselves in Mickey, admired and aspired to be like him—grit, playing through pain, exceptional performance. Yet Mickey never desired the role-model attention, found it uncomfortable because of the way he thought of himself. A man of a thousand feats as well as a thousand cracks and disappointments.

The good, the bad, the selfish, the selfless, the piteous, the self-piteous, the cruel, the clever, the kind, the unkind, the cursed, the conflicted, the simple, the shrewd, the destructive, the self-destructive, the haunted, the hunted, the gifted, the great, the natural, the supernatural. Mantle was all of it. If you read Jane Leavy's book *The Last Boy*—and you should, as it is one of the best works

of sports reportage ever—Mantle's image of himself, so turned inside out by his demons, never found a permanent reconciliation except at the end of his life.

His moods could go from zero to sixty in five seconds, and his wife, Merlyn, thought he might be manic-depressive. He attacked watercoolers with special vengeance. He had a great sense of humor and razor-quick wit, but there was often an edge of nastiness to his penchant for juvenile pranks. His relationship with fans was never a constant love affair. He grew to love Merlyn unlike any other woman, but he routinely cheated on her and humiliated her and finally separated from her. He barely was with his children as they grew up. When his first son was born he waited two months to see him because it was spring training. And yet he cried with unbridled sentimentality after he saw *The Last Picture Show*, a depiction of small-town life with a single traffic light swinging in the ceaseless dust-infested wind, reminding him of his own upbringing in the relentless grimness of Commerce, Oklahoma. He could be inordinately kind, whether it was a homeless person freezing in the tony streets of New York's Upper East Side or a Yankee rookie terrified of failure in the greatest sports franchise in the world. He could be surly and sour after his career when a ten-year-old politely asked for his autograph, Mickey sadly infected with the booze that ultimately turned his liver into a dying mass of scab.

He enthralled on the field, but he failed to rehabilitate from injuries in the off-season. There were nagging questions as to why he had been declared 4-F and therefore exempt from the draft

Casey Stengal instructing a
young Mantle at spring training,
St. Petersburg, Florida, 1953

during the Korean War. He never got past the happiest times of his life, boys being boys in the sanctity of the clubhouse, playing what will always be a boys' game.

As Bob Costas, a very close friend of Mantle's, told me, "The flawed and the tragic often attract us more than the successful." His appeal, said Costas, was a "combination of the person and the context of the fifties and sixties when baseball was different, still the national pastime. There was the greatness of the Yankees, and Mickey's dynamism of natural speed and natural power. There was also the star-crossed nature of it, what might have been."

Being followed by young fans
outside Yankee Stadium, 1956

Mantle was the American Dream and the American complication, a movie codirected by Frank Capra, Quentin Tarantino,
Oliver Stone, and Steven Spielberg. His life was out of Steinbeck—
his humble upbringing in the mining hellholes of northeastern
Oklahoma, the father who worked in the devil's patch of those
underground mines and willed his son to become a baseball player
to avoid the pitilessness of his own life. There was the discovery
of him in the middle of nowhere in Commerce by legendary Yankee scout Tom Greenwade; the meteoric move to New York in
1951 after only two years in the minors, with a pair of shoes and

Entering a hotel lobby in St.
Petersburg, Florida, 1953

FOLLOWING: Driving a tractor on
a practice field, St. Petersburg,
Florida, 1953

a single tie with an animal on it that someone had given to him; the instantaneous pressure and expectation placed upon him as a worthy successor to the great DiMaggio. Even the name itself evoked something different.

Steve Mantle? John Mantle? Joe Mantle? It had to be Mickey, Mickey Mantle, named after the great catcher for the Philadelphia A's Mickey Cochrane. Alliterative. Compact. One hundred percent American like another American icon, Mickey Mouse. Wholly unique, like everything Mantle did. No compromise. No halfway gesture. No holding back, cutting himself open in every facet of his life, a public operating table.

He wasn't a legend just because of his baseball feats. He also was a legend because of that humanity, a man who taught us to live by making himself an example of how not to live, and a man who taught us all how to die.

Would his reputation have been different today? Of course it would have been, his late-night peccadilloes the stuff of the back page of the *New York Post* for weeks on end. But the trivial yet voracious sensationalism that exists now, the American craving of celebrity in which private lives are far more important than public performance, did not exist then. His off-field activities, shredded by the bottom-feeding gossip suckerfish feeding on silt, would have brutalized him.

Thank God he wasn't alive for it. Thank God he could always be The Mick.

Portrait of Mantle, 1956

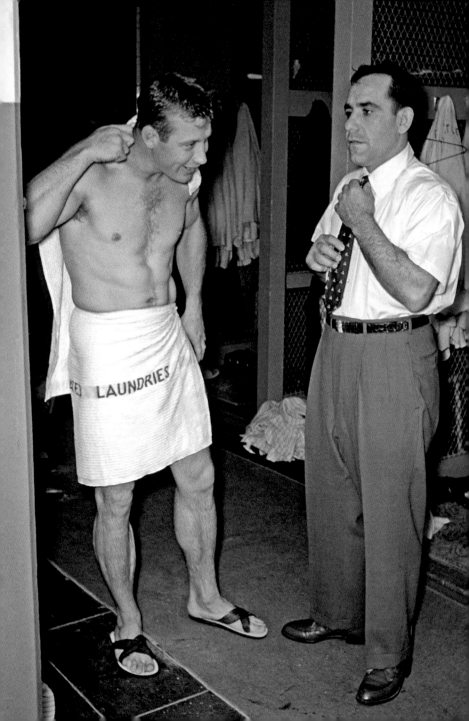

I lived and died with my Yankees, rose

and fell with them, laughed in joy with them during the few times in childhood when I expressed genuine joy. I still remember the catch Bobby Richardson made of the shot-out-of-a-cannon line drive by Willie McCovey with men on second and third to win the seventh game of the 1962 World Series against the Giants, 1–0. I shed too many tears in the humiliating World Series sweep by the Los Angeles Dodgers in 1963, appropriating the swagger that had once been owned by the Yankees for more than forty years. But a confession:

As much as Mickey Mantle held me in a trance, he was not my favorite player. Not right away.

I am not sure why, since my father and grandfather and uncle, all Yankee fans themselves, pontificated on his greatness over and over. The Yankees were still the bomb in the 1960s when I became of true baseball age, at least until 1965, when the bottom finally fell out and they went eleven years without another World Series appearance.

During the span of my lifetime from 1954 until 1965, they had

Mantle with Yogi Berra, shown
dressing in the Yankee Stadium
locker room after a shower, 1955

won those twelve pennants and seven World Series and Mantle had been there for all of it when he wasn't hurt. But he did not rouse me the most as a child. When the first signs of my Yankee fanaticism revealed themselves, in 1960, it was someone else who held the biggest piece of my heart.

I loved Bobby Richardson because he seemed so quiet and controlled and efficient without ever drawing attention to himself. Baseball cards were just baseball cards back then—you didn't wear a pair of white, sanitized surgical gloves in an air-locked room free of dust when you opened them, and you didn't go into apoplectic shock if you bent one of the corners. The rectangular sticks of pink bubble gum that stuck to the cards were added bonuses, leaving a residue of white sweetness you sometimes licked if very hungry. Getting a Topps Mantle card was a big deal, but then I usually piled it away in a brown shopping bag. It never made the sacred, small stack neatly wrapped in a rubber band. World Series cards were the best, and I spent hours looking at Game 3 from the 1960 World Series when Richardson, the ultimate nonpower hitter, hit a grand slam and drove in a record six runs. I liked Elston Howard because he was elegant and classy. I liked the left-handed Johnny Blanchard because he hit 21 dingers in 1961 in 243 at-bats, which made him an almost automatic home run against righties if you played Strat-O-Matic baseball.

I liked underdogs, maybe because of my own penchant for the melancholic. In 1961, when Mantle and Roger Maris battled each other to top the sacred record of 60 home runs set by Ruth in 1927,

I always rooted for Maris. Mickey may have been from nowhere Oklahoma, but at least the state had a musical named after it. Roger was from North Dakota, a state that had nothing except that it was kind of close to Wall Drug, in neighboring South Dakota. I spent time in Fargo, where Maris grew up, since my grandfather lived relatively close by, across the Minnesota border. People were gracious and friendly, but it was still the kind of place where no matter how many people you went out with to dinner, you still felt like the only person at the table. I kept thinking of him spending his formative years walking through snow and ice with the wind

Mickey Mantle, Enos Slaughter, and
Yogi Berra by the batting cage at
the Brooklyn World Series, 1956

blowing off the prairie like sheets of steel, and ending up in New York seemed cruel and unusual punishment for a man of such obvious privacy.

It was another perspective from the eyes of a child—I was only six at the time—but Mantle just seemed to be having a ball as he rose to 54 home runs before an injury sidetracked him for roughly the last two weeks of the season. Now on his own in pursuit of the holy grail of baseball records, Maris lost hair, smoked three packs of Camels a day, snarled at reporters, and was not particularly liked by fans who felt that it was Mickey who really deserved the record or, in the alternative, that Maris had no business encroaching upon the Babe. Yankee fans were extreme and snobby purists. We could afford to be, I guess. We weren't the Evil Empire then. We were the Empire.

When Maris did break Ruth's record on the last day of the regular season, against the Boston Red Sox's Tracy Stallard, hitting a fourth-inning pitch on the outside corner several rows back into the right-field stands, it was hard to tell if he felt euphoria, relief, vindication, or the kind of taciturn fatalism seemingly all people from North Dakota have that life might not get any worse but it was not going to get any better, not with that wind forever whistling in your ear. Even Mantle, who went out of his way to embrace Maris and take him under his wing, realized with his country wisdom (he was always much smarter than people thought) that Maris had lost the home run race even though he had won, and Mantle himself had won it even though he had lost. Rogers Hornsby called Maris

Being congratulated by Elston Howard for a World Series home run at Yankee Stadium, 1956

a "punk baseball player." Sportswriter Jimmy Cannon said he was a "whiner."

"I became an American hero in 1961 because he beat me," Mantle later said. "He was an ass, and I was a nice guy. He beat Babe Ruth, and he beat me, so they hated him. Everywhere we'd go, I got a standing ovation. All I had to do was walk out of the dugout."

Mantle was given several injections for the injury that took him out of the battle for Ruth, thought initially to be a virulent flu. One of them became infected, creating a hole in his buttocks about the size of a golf ball, maybe even bigger, that oozed blood and pus and required hospitalization. It was excruciating to the touch. He did not appear in the first two games of the 1961 World Series, against the Cincinnati Reds; typically he insisted on playing despite the agony of every at-bat. Leading off the second inning of the fourth game, Mantle hit a groundball to third. He was only partway to first base when the wound pulled apart and he began to bleed. He tried to hide it with his glove when he returned to the dugout, downplaying it as no big deal until Yankee manager Ralph Houk saw the blood all over the place. And yet, even though Mickey could barely run, he still went to bat in the fourth. He hit a 2-and-1 pitch from the Reds' Jim O'Toole into the gap that normally would have been an easy double. But Mantle had to stop at first, his leg a bloody mess. Everybody could see it. He was lifted for a pinch runner and received a standing ovation from his Yankee teammates. Even O'Toole couldn't quite believe that Mantle had done it. "God bless him," he said. Whatever could be said of Mantle, the one element never disputed was

Rounding third base at Fenway Park, 1954

his absolute toughness. Teammate after teammate attested to it, the acceptance of pain however severe. He always wanted to be on the baseball field. It was the closest he ever had to a home.

Playing through the injury in the 1961 World Series, won by the Yankees in five games, just added to the existing legend of Mantle. The 1961 season marked a crucial shift in his career, changing the fickle attitude of Yankee fans about him. They revered him again.

It hadn't always been that way.

It seemed nonsensical for any Yankee fan to ever be down on Mantle—until you read some of the newspaper accounts when he came up to the Bronx Bombers in 1951 after the spring exhibition season, during which he batted .402 and hit nine home runs. Wrote one scribe who immediately thereafter probably died of sportswriterly hyperinflation, "If the inking device on the Fordham University seismograph didn't trace a design like a cross section of Mount Everest set in the middle of the American Prairies, it's a fraud because Mickey Mantle, the rookie of the aeons, hit New York like fifteen simultaneous earthquakes." Another called him "The Sweet Switcher."

The *New York Times Magazine* did a profile on him, noting that he was already being memorialized in poem by adoring fans. Not even Jesus could have met all the expectations. No matter what Mickey did, and he did so much, there was always a collective gluttony from fans to front office that they still needed more. Is it possible for someone to have too much talent?

Maybe for Mickey Mantle.

At the Pittsburgh World Series,
Heinz Field, 1960

FOLLOWING: Batting right-handed,
Yankee Stadium, 1956

Beginning with his very first star-crossed year in the major leagues, 1951, the decade was a clash of contradictions for Mantle. There were periods of both greatness and disappointment. There were periods in which fans could not get enough of him and periods in which fans, particularly in the late 1950s, had more than enough of him. His crescent moon smile diminished in those low ebbs, replaced by sullenness and rages of frustration and grunts and groans with reporters. There was the temptation of New York with its women and nightclubs as well as the nightmare of New York with its women and nightclubs. He drank too much and he partied too much into the wee hours of the morning, and he knew it. There was the ghost always lurking that he felt he had let too many people down.

There is a scene in the film *Friday Night Lights* where the quarterback Mike Winchell, from a hermetic and isolated town in West Texas, much like Mantle was from a hermetic and isolated town in Oklahoma, tries to grapple with success versus the insecurity of what he believes will always be inevitable failure.

"You ever feel cursed, Coach? Like, no matter what, inside your heart you feel that you're gonna lose. Like something's hanging over you, following you like a witch or a demon that just . . . I feel like that all the time. Even when things are going good. When we're winnin', it's there. And when we're losin', it's there."

Those lines always remind me of Mantle. He may have been a country boy who crossed into Missouri to Joplin for excitement, but his talent was unlike anything anyone had ever seen, his power an

Tossing his glove between innings
in center field at Yankee Stadium,
1954

anomaly because of a diminutive frame of 5-11 and 190 pounds. Power hitters in the big leagues were typically big, hefty, lumbering. Mantle was all compaction, as if every muscle worked in perfect and optimal unison. Starting from the left-handed batter's box when nobody knew who he was, he made it to first base in an unheard-of 2.9 seconds. Yankee manager Casey Stengel was so shocked he made him do it again. So he did it again. His power from both sides of the plate was unprecedented. In spring training in 1951, with the Yankees in Phoenix, and with Mickey coming up from lowly C-level ball, Stengel, usually caustic and reticent in his evaluation of players, branded the tag of "can't miss" on his forehead after watching him play. "He has more speed than any slugger and more slug than any speedster—and nobody has ever had more of both of 'em together."

The elevation to greatness came during spring training when the Yankees played an exhibition game at the University of Southern California. Batting from the left side, Mickey hit a home run that some say traveled 656 feet (when the man becomes a legend, print the legend). Then he hit a second, from the right side, well over 500 feet, that landed on top of a three-story house.

Sportswriters leapfrogged over each other to come up with the pithiest description: "Commerce Comet," "Colossal Kid," "Wonder Boy," "The Future of Baseball," and my personal favorite, "Young Lochinvar" (memorialized in the poem *Marmion* by Sir Walter Scott in 1808).

The talent was so clearly there, beyond there, beyond *any-*

Running to first base at a night
game, Yankee Stadium, 1955

thing. The only flaw was that he came up playing shortstop in the minors, where he made fifty-five errors one season. But the Yankee front office knew he was a good enough athlete to convert into an outfielder. They had no control over the natural insecurities of a nineteen-year-old suddenly starting in right field for the Yankees and being heralded as the imminent replacement for the great DiMaggio. The poundings of instant mortality made him uncomfortable with interviews, although even then he was wise enough to know that the minute the press stopped bothering him with questions, "then you start to worry."

But he was fundamentally naive and impulsive and always too trusting, entering into terrible deals for representation in which he never consulted with seasoned teammates. Far more debilitating was the curse of freak injury that during his career included two operations on his right knee after blowing it out, a removal of a cyst behind the knee, a strained right thigh muscle in four different seasons, a fractured right index finger, an abscess in the right hip, shin splints, loose cartilage removed from the left knee, a broken metatarsus, an injured right shoulder that he reinjured a season later, a pulled muscle in the left thigh, and a strained right hamstring.

He played well in his rookie year of 1951. He was leading the team in RBIs, a strong candidate for American League Rookie of the Year. But Stengel, whether out of genuine concern or an attempt

Hitting the ball, Yankee Stadium, 1955

to put Mantle in his place so the ego didn't balloon, said he was striking out too much. He was sent down to the Yankees' AAA American Association franchise, the Kansas City Blues, in July to make way for pitcher Art Schallock (who won three games for the Yankees in four seasons).

Mantle sobbed when he left, convinced that this was his only shot with the Yankees and he had blown it. He slumped badly with the Blues initially, and his attraction to the high life, drinking and ordering caviar even though he probably didn't know what caviar was, didn't help.

In desperation he called his father, Mutt, and told him he wanted to come home. A book alone could be written about the relationship between son Mickey and father Mutt with its oedipal overtones. Freud would have danced a jig, a new book on psychoanalysis called *Mickey and Mutt: The Complex of Complete Muddle*. He pushed his son mercilessly, ordaining him from birth in 1931 that he was going to be a baseball player. The son lived in awe of his father, loving him, scared of him, taking every lead from him, always convinced that he was never meeting the standard the father had set, helpless without him but helpless with him because he never fully formed, his life on autopilot since Mutt always figured the next move. Mutt, not wanting Mickey to replicate his own life of working in the mines, loved his son and also clearly lived through him once he got the whiff that he had a superior athlete on his hands.

There was mercy in that, given the conditions of Picher

Mantle at bat and Berra on deck,
spring training, St. Petersburg,
Florida, 1953

Field, where Mutt worked. Zinc and lead were the mother lodes, but to get to them in the belowground shafts in the 1920s, at least 173 miners were killed, mostly from falling rock, according to Leavy's book. There was also the rampant threat of tuberculosis and silicosis. Between 1927 and 1932, wrote Leavy, more than 5,000 of 30,000 miners who were examined had both diseases. But the examinations were for the benefit of the mine operators, not the miners. If an X-ray came back positive, the miner was immediately fired and blackballed from mine work ever again anywhere. As an attorney for one of the companies, Eagle-Picher,

Mantle on third base getting instructions from coach Frank Crosetti, 1953

put it, "When they get sick and can't work, we throw them on the dump heap."

The son certified the father in a life defined by such unforgiving work. The father certified the son not with open love—the father never once told the son he loved him—but with the fanatical hours he spent to make him the best baseball player he could possibly be.

Without the father, it is doubtful the son would have been as great as he was. But Mickey's insecurities, his lack of confidence, his ultimate destructiveness and self-immolation, were at the very least a partial legacy of Mutt as well. He was demanding. He was critical. When they practiced for hours every afternoon, Mutt ignored Mickey's expressions of hunger for dinner as whining. He sometimes threw one at his head just to make sure he was paying attention. Mickey lived in fear; he wet his bed until he was sixteen. Some believe that he married hometown girl Merlyn more out of love and respect for his father than for Merlyn herself. Mutt thought Merlyn was right for Mickey, and that was that. But they weren't ready to get married.

When they went on their honeymoon, Mickey invited another couple, as if he were scared to be alone with Merlyn. When they lived together in New York for the first time, holed up in the Concourse Plaza Hotel near Yankee Stadium in what Merlyn described as a "tiny, bleak room [with] a bed, a chair, one closet, and a bathroom" but no television because it cost $10 a month, she might as well have gone to live on Saturn.

But Mutt did take great pride in his son. He relentlessly pushed him because he knew that life in the misery of northeastern Oklahoma was no life at all. Back in Commerce after his son made the show, he loved to brag about Mickey. He told people that Mickey and Joe DiMaggio were friends, even though DiMaggio barely ever said a word to him and to the contrary went out of his way to snub Mantle and forever resented his presence, throwing fits if he felt the remotest possibility that Mickey might upstage him.

Mutt came up to see his son in Kansas City right after the phone call. Mickey was relieved and glad to see him. "I wanted him to pat me on the back and cheer me up and tell me how badly the Yankees had treated me and all that sort of stuff. . . . I wanted him to comfort me," said Mantle. There are many versions of the story, like there are many versions of every Mantle story. It's like trying to establish the exact truth in a dime novel about the Wild West. But the consensus is that Mutt called his son a "goddamn coward" and a "baby" and told him "You ain't got a gut in your body." He started throwing the son's possessions into a bag and said he was going to take him back to Commerce, where a job in the hellholes awaited him.

Mickey cried as any nineteen-year-old would have, but Mutt's challenge to his manhood did have the desired effect: He stayed. He began to hit and by the end of the summer was back in New York after roughly a five-week absence. He returned with typical

Being congratulated on hitting
a home run at Pittsburgh, World
Series, 1960

Mantle panache, clubbing a home run against the Cleveland Indians and hitting .274 the rest of the season. The rudiments of greatness began to show, and it was only a matter of time before you could drop the "rudiments" part. Mantle, Willie Mays, and Hank Aaron were destined to become the next generation of superstar players. Mays and Aaron *were* great; they both had more consistent careers than Mickey. They were both obvious Hall of Famers. They both had more home runs than Mantle over their careers and finished with batting averages over .300. They both played in an environment where African American players were still not accepted, whereas Mantle obviously never had to face any racism. But it was Mantle and Mantle alone who did things on the baseball field that were not simply spectacular but also crossed the line into the world of the surreal, the unfathomable. How could anybody hit a ball that hard? And be that fast? And be that tough? And be that charming when he wanted to be, the king of New York even though he might as well have been born a million miles away.

Mantle finished his first season with a .267 average and .349 on-base percentage and 13 home runs in 96 contests. The Yankees won the pennant by five games over the Cleveland Indians to face off against the New York Giants. The Giants were on adrenalized air, making it to the Series on Bobby Thomson's ninth-inning home run off the Brooklyn Dodgers' Ralph Branca in the deciding game of a three-game playoff. Mantle batted leadoff in the first game. He went 0 for 3 in a 5–1 loss to the Giants.

Then the disaster.

Batting right-handed, Yankee
Stadium, 1956

It occurred in the top of the fifth of the second game when Willie Mays hit a blooper into right center. Yankee manager Casey Stengel had told Mantle to charge as hard as he could into DiMaggio's domain, since he had lost a step. Mantle obeyed the order. But when he got to the ball, DiMaggio was there. The last thing Mantle wanted to do as a rookie was crash into DiMaggio. *I'm gonna hit DiMaggio*, he thought. *I'll put him in the hospital. They'll never let me play again.*

He pulled up.

His back cleat got caught on the rubber cover of a drain hole concealed by the grass. His knee shot out in front of his right leg; a bone was sticking out. He crumpled and didn't move, and some thought he might have gotten shot. Although nobody knew it at the time—MRIs and arthroscopic surgery did not exist—Mantle had destroyed his knee in three areas.

The knee became so swollen that he went to Lenox Hill Hospital the next day and was there for the remainder of the Series (the Yankees won in six games). Despite medical treatment, the pain lingered, often like fire. He still had blazing speed, but he had lost lateral movement. He also knew that as long as he played baseball, he would never be the same. "That October afternoon was the last time Mantle set foot on a baseball field without pain," Leavy wrote. "He would play the next seventeen years struggling to be as good as he could be, knowing he would never be as good as he might have become."

Something else happened at that moment, freakish because

Batting in slow motion, Yankee
Stadium, 1955

of the timing and of far more import. His father was in the stands when his son was hurt; he took him to Lenox Hill because of the swelling. Mickey could barely walk, so he used Mutt as a crutch. Mutt, normally so strong, collapsed under the weight. Mickey fell to the sidewalk as well. They both ended up in the same hospital room, where the son ultimately found out the reason for his father's weakness:

He had Hodgkin's disease.

Less than a year later, Mutt Mantle died on May 6, 1952, at age forty. He was buried at the Grand Army of the Republic Cemetery

Follow through after hitting a home
run, Yankee Stadium, 1956

in Ottawa County in Oklahoma. The plot, to the right of gate 2, was spare and simple, a small rectangle recording Mutt's year of birth and year of death.

If his father had terrified Mickey, the only thing that terrified him *more* was Mutt's absence. Mickey was on his own now. There was no governor now to stop his bad judgment and curtail his excess and tell him exactly what to do. For all his famous rabble-rousing, for all his love of the clubhouse, loneliness overwhelmed him, a man on top of the world and at the bottom of it at the very same time. Beloved over time by so many millions except for himself. Uncomfortable with the compliments because they embarrassed him. A great drinking companion until it morphed into alcoholic anger and self-pity. A sense of humor at its best when he aimed the jabs squarely at himself.

But God, could he still play baseball.

In 1952, his second season, he hit .311,

the first of ten seasons in which he would hit over .300. In the World Series that year, won by the Yankees in seven games over the Brooklyn Dodgers, Mantle established his penchant for postseason clutch with 10 hits in 29 at-bats, including 2 home runs, a triple, and a double. In the final and deciding game, a 4–2 win before 33,195 at Ebbets Field, Mantle hit a single shot in the sixth off Joe Black to give the Yanks a 3–2 lead, then singled in the seventh off Preacher Roe to drive in the insurance run.

In the clubhouse celebration afterward, Mantle stood next to Gene Woodling. The peak of Mickey's cap was turned up and wisps of hair were matted to his forehead. The smile on his face was soft and serene. You could see the perfect alignment of white teeth and the soft eyes and the bull neck belonging to someone who was all of twenty years old. He was as all-American as apple and pecan and cherry pie put together under one giant crust. He was boyish and beautiful.

The legend had only just begun.

In 1953, he hit a home run over the right-field roof of Forbes

At-bat pose, Yankee Stadium, 1955   PREVIOUS: Clowning around on the
grass at Yankee Stadium, 1956

Field batting *left-handed* in an exhibition game against the Pittsburgh Pirates. The following week, on April 17, the Yankees played the Washington Senators in the fourth game of the regular season. It was a Friday. All of 4,206 fans showed up in the 35,000-seat Griffith Stadium in the nation's capital. With two outs in the fifth, Mantle, batting *right-handed*, faced Chuck Stobbs. With a favorable wind, with gusts as high as 40 miles an hour, Mantle made contact with the ball. Aided by the jet stream, the ball soared and soared and soared. . . .

It went over a 50-foot-high wall at the back of the left-center bleachers, traveling an estimated 460 feet on the fly. It clipped the football scoreboard, then just kept going, landing somewhere in the vicinity of Fifth Street. Immediately the Yankees' director of public relations, Arthur E. Patterson, leaped into action because this was a baseball moment that might never be equaled. Patterson left Griffith Stadium, used paces as a measuring stick, and determined that the ball had been hit 565 feet, the longest in the history of baseball. Later studies by eminent physicists estimated the actual flight between 506 feet and 540 feet. Close enough.

Mickey made the cover of *Time* in June 1953 at a time when an 80-mile-per-hour fastball was described as a "bullet" and owners fretted over the device called television. "Young Man on Olympus," read the headline, and the writer described watching Mantle in an at-bat against Billy Pierce of the Chicago White Sox:

"Mickey Mantle set a muscular chain in motion. Starting in the ankles, rippling through knees, hips, torso, broad shoulders

and 17-inch bull neck, he brought his bat around in a perfect arc to meet the ball with a sharp crack. High and deep it sailed. The White Sox center fielder, playing deep, went a few steps back, then stood, face upturned, as the ball sailed over the fence for a 425-foot home run."

The writer was just revving up the motor.

"Like Ruth, Mickey hits towering homers. Like Ted Williams, he smacks crackling line drives. Like DiMaggio, he beats out hot-to-handle grounders if an infielder makes a split-second bobble."

Ruth. Williams. DiMaggio. The only player missing was Gehrig.

The more Mickey Mantle did, the more he needed to do.

He did.

In 1956 he went wild. The first game of the season, against the poor Senators, was an omen of things to come as Mantle connected for two homers with President Dwight Eisenhower in attendance. On June 18, against the Detroit Tigers, Mickey hit a ball out of Briggs Stadium; only Ted Williams had done that before, but Mantle's shot was 20 to 30 feet longer. He drew record crowds on the road, established himself as the best player in the league, and the superlatives that would torture him all his life once again came out: Former Yankee catcher Bill Dickey predicted that he would break every Yankee record except for Gehrig's consecutive-game mark of 2,130. Former New York Giants superstar Mel Ott said that Mantle could well finish the season with 75 home runs and more

than 190 RBIs, both major league records. At the All-Star break he had 29 homers and was batting .371. He dropped a little bit in the second half, but won the Triple Crown with a batting average of .353, 52 home runs, and 130 runs batted in. He also led the American League in runs scored with 132, an OPS of 1.169, and a slugging percentage of .705. As an added bonus, he was 10 for 11 stealing.

His career was still nascent; it was only his sixth season. He was twenty-four years old. How could anyone this young be that good? Forget *good*. That great? Forget *great*. That brilliant? Forget *brilliant*. There wasn't a proper word.

Running home at a night game,
Yankee Stadium

But 1956 also became a noose, the expectation that every season would be just like it. In 1957 he hit .365 and had an on-base percentage of .512. But nobody particularly cared about on-base percentage back then, and Mantle's home runs (34) and RBIs (94) were significantly down. In 1958 he led the American League in home runs with 42, but his batting average had dropped to .304; while he led the league in walks (129), he also led in strikeouts (120). The 1959 season was only worse, an unmitigated disaster for the Yankees and for Mantle. For the second time in his career, the Yankees did not win the pennant, falling to the Chicago White Sox.

The exploits of 1956 seemed further and further removed, and more and more people believed it was due to Mantle's too-often surly temperament and his refusal to rehabilitate from all those injuries in the off-season. There also was an inkling of his drinking and partying with the famous Copacabana melee on May 16, 1957, attended by several Yankees, including Mantle, Billy Martin, and Hank Bauer. Charges were filed and then dismissed. But the Yankees believed Martin to be such a bad influence on Mantle that they traded him to Kansas City shortly afterward.

The trade of Martin didn't seem to help, or at least not help as much as the Yankees thought it would. Yankee manager Casey Stengel, who liked to praise Mantle and then verbally stab him in the stomach much like Mickey's father, became more and more derisive.

"This kid still has everything and he has a lot of career ahead of him, that is if he don't screw up, and he comes close to screw-

With roommate Billy Martin outside
the Edison Hotel in New York City,
1955

ing up every goddamned day of his life," said Stengel. "In the first place he has little sense about people, and I'm always worried if he's going to buy the Brooklyn Bridge."

George Weiss, the famously cheap general manager of the Yankees, said he never had a player "who was the subject of as much discussion and analysis" in a story in the *Saturday Evening Post* on the eve of the 1960 season. "Our entire organization has tried to discover why Mantle hasn't capitalized on his enormous potential, and we obviously haven't found the answer.

"Physically, Mantle has the attributes of a superstar, a blend of Babe Ruth and Ty Cobb. He is much faster than DiMaggio was and he has more power, with the added advantage of being a switch-hitter and getting the benefit of the short right-field fence in the Stadium. . . . Add up Mantle's assets, and he's superior to DiMaggio, but he hasn't come close to proving it yet."

It was as if the 1956 Triple Crown season had never existed. What was wrong with Mickey Mantle? It became a preoccupation among writers, an endless Rorschach. Was it his brutally demanding father? Was it the fear of death that became public when he told Howard Cosell he was convinced he was living on borrowed time given that his father, grandfather, and uncle had all died of Hodgkin's in their early forties? Because of Cosell, the image of Mantle as the doomed player with death hanging over him became repeated over and over, to the point of melodramatic cliché.

He was still the toast of New York, both because of his celebrated swing and because he probably had made a toast or two or

Preparing to bat at Yankee Stadium, 1955

three in every swanky bar in New York, Toots Shor's his favorite. But there were fissures. Yankee fans were too used to winning. And there were some who decided that Mantle was a sour bum, with none of the class and fluid elegance of the great DiMaggio.

In an article in the *New York Times* on June 1, 1958, Gay Talese noted that Mantle was more popular away than he was at home. The previous Friday, in a doubleheader with the Senators, wrote Talese, "A girl of thirteen jumped at Mantle as he got out of the cab. She punched him, began to pull his short, blond hair, and slapped him. He swatted her off and bulldozed his way toward the Stadium's player-entrance."

The incident was an extreme, but as Talese noted, it was not unusual for teenagers to squirt ink on Mantle's clothing if he did not sign autographs. The day Talese surveyed the Stadium, one fan said of Mantle from the bleachers during batting practice, "Look, here comes the All-American Out." Another screamed, "Mantle, you couldn't play on the Bushwicks [a semipro team that had played in Queens]." You had to hand it to Mantle haters: They were sharp and cunning in their cruelty. Some fans believed he was stuck-up when he still was what he always had been—a reticent kid from Oklahoma comfortable only with his teammates. Others resented the amount of money he was making. Others had never forgiven him for being classified as 4-F by the army, convinced he had gotten favorable treatment despite three exhaustive medical examinations. "Maybe it's because we expect too much from Mantle," thirty-seven-year-old Mike Rich, from Bayonne, New

Rounding third base for home, World Series versus the Dodgers, 1956

FOLLOWING: Hank Bauer, Tom Sturdivant, and Mickey Mantle after World Series Game 4, 1956

Jersey, told Talese. "He's been getting booed since he came to the Stadium. He got too much publicity when he first came out here."

The booing got worse in the disastrous season of 1959. Stengel was getting increasingly cranky and insulting. He exerted less and less influence, and Jackie Robinson said there were rumors that Stengel was napping during games. The team itself was old blood desperate for an infusion of new blood. Much of the venting by the fans was taken out on Mantle. In a losing game to the Detroit Tigers, he hit a home run off Frank Lary and was booed. Normally Mickey vented his rage at watercoolers, but he began to make obscene gestures to fans who were riding him.

He hit only .285 that year, his worst season averagewise since his rookie year. He hit 31 home runs and drove in 75, and his strikeouts were a career-high and league-high 126. Baseball was different back then. Players were treated as chattels, living on year-to-year contracts instead of the multiyear, multimillion-dollar deals they get now, in which some, long after they have stopped playing, still get paid because of deferred compensation. (See Bobby Bonilla, who although he hasn't played for the New York Mets in fifteen years, is still getting paid roughly $1.2 million a year. Or Gary Sheffield, whom the Detroit Tigers owe between $1 million and $2.5 million a year until 2019. Or Ken Griffey Jr., who will be paid roughly $3.5 million a year by the Cincinnati Reds until 2025.)

Weiss wanted to cut Mantle's salary by $17,000. Mantle held out and the cut was $7,000, to $65,000 (Mantle got paid roughly

$1 million in salary during his entire career, 50 percent less than what Bonilla is getting each year for not touching the field).

During spring training in 1960, as noted in David Faulkner's book *The Last Hero*, there was a yacht party among various players during which the boat caught fire. Mantle could not even swim, but rescuers managed to save him.

The 1960 season felt like a replay of 1959, a man on a snowball slide. But Jane Leavy believes that the turning point for Mantle came in mid-August 1960. It started miserably enough, during the second game of a doubleheader loss to yes, you guessed it, the

Running to first base, 1956

Senators. Mantle hit a double-play ball in the seventh with the game tied 3–3; livid with himself and once again trying to play through injury (more ligament damage to his right knee), he didn't even bother to run it out. The inning was over and the booing came down like pouring rain. In an act of obvious public humiliation, Mantle stayed on the field, waiting for a teammate to bring him his glove, when Stengel very publicly replaced him with Bob Cerv. Stengel said afterward, "It didn't look very good, us trying to win when the man hits the ball to second . . . and doesn't run it out. That's not the first time he's done that. If he can't run, he should tell me. If he wants to come out, all he has to do is tell me. Who the hell does he think he is, Superman?" Not even his own teammates could find a way to defend what he had done. You could party all night, you could play hungover or pray that Casey would not make you play because you were hungover. But you always ran to first.

Arguably it was the lowest point of Mantle's career. The loss dropped the Yankees into a first-place tie with the Orioles, their next opponent, on August 15. When Mantle came to the plate for his first at-bat at Yankee Stadium before 24,233, the booing was even worse than it had been the day before, against the Senators. He responded by grounding out to first. But he tied the game in the fourth inning with a two-run homer, driving in Hector Lopez. With the Orioles ahead 3–2 in the eighth, Mantle homered again with Lopez on to give the Yankees a 4–3 victory.

It was a one-for-the-ages turnaround for Mantle (given the endless games of today, it was perhaps even more magical that

Mantle, Stengel, and Berra at
spring training, St. Petersburg,
Florida, 1953

Yankee pitcher Art Ditmar pitched a complete game; the Orioles used only two pitchers and the contest was played four minutes shy of two hours). The raucous boos turned into raucous cheers. The rehabilitation of Mantle in the eyes of fans had begun, further reinforced a year later in the home run derby with Maris.

Mantle methodically crept into my heart.

In 1963 the Yanks played the Kansas City A's. Eddie Lopat, the A's manager, who for some reason thought it made strategic sense to trash-mouth Mantle, yelled to him from the dugout as he came to the plate from the left side, "You got no bat speed. You can't get

Mickey Mantle with manager
Casey Stengel, spring training,
St. Petersburg, Florida, 1953

ABOVE: Mantle on first base with Gil
Hodges, the Brooklyn first baseman,
World Series, 1956

it out of the outfield. You were up too late last night." Mantle stared at Lopat; the artery was bulging in the side of Mickey's neck.

The ball traveled approximately 367 feet in length and 108 feet in height before hitting the copper frieze above the third deck in right field. The inevitable aeronautical estimates came out: the ball traveled at 123 miles an hour and would have gone about 620 feet had it not hit the frieze. Yankee third baseman Clete Boyer probably put it best when he said, "That's a three-dollar cab ride up there," as much a comment about inflation as it was about speed and distance.

Plagued by injuries, Mantle played in only 65 games that season, and 1963 was ruined anyway by that embarrassing four-game sweep by the Dodgers, with a starting pitching staff led by Sandy Koufax, Don Drysdale, and Johnny Podres. Mantle did homer in the fourth game to tie the score at 1—1, and Whitey Ford went seven innings and gave up only two hits. But in the bottom of the seventh, first baseman Joe Pepitone lost a routine throw from third baseman Clete Boyer in the white shirts of the crowd for a three-base error and ultimately the winning run. The Yankees managed 22 hits in the entire Series. I was in third grade at the time, and the only positive to come out of the mess was the dignified restraint of classmate Nancy Fuld, a fanatical fan of West Coast teams. She could sense I was on the brink of violence at the remotest sign of razzing.

It was in the third game of the 1964 World Series, against the St. Louis Cardinals, when Mantle finally stole my heart.

I was watching the game on television when he faced reliever Barney Schultz in the bottom of the ninth inning with the score tied, 1–1. It was perhaps the greatest first-name match-up in the history of baseball, Mick versus Barney, Barney versus Mick. It was also agony, one of those games where my eyes were shut half the time and I kept praying for a miracle, although I wasn't quite sure to whom I was praying, given the nonreligiousness of my family. Mantle led off the inning, and nailed Schultz's offering into the right-field porch of Yankee Stadium to win the game. He had a good Series that year despite the Yankees losing in the decisive seventh game. He hit three home runs and drove in eight.

But it was his swan song of greatness. The 1965 season was one of great struggle for him and the Yankees in general as the dynasty crumbled. In one of the oddest baseball moves ever, the Yankees had fired Yogi Berra as manager after losing the World Series, replacing him with Johnny Keane, who had just won the World Series with the Cardinals. Keane was a strict disciplinarian who was appointed by the front office to curb the Yankees' late-night forays. He and Mantle sparred from the very beginning. During spring training, angry that Mantle was hungover, Keane ordered him to go into center field and then took out a fungo bat and hit fifty balls, according to Faulkner's book. "He was trying to make me sick," said Mantle, and at one point Mantle caught a fly and threw it as hard as he could directly at Keane. He missed, and he knew he should apologize, but he never did. He was right. Keane was a fossil.

The Yankees finished sixth in 1965 with a 77-85 record, their first losing season in forty years, 25 games behind the pennant-winning Minnesota Twins. The core of the team was still there. But it was rotted with age and lack of youth and overfamiliarity—Howard, Maris, Richardson, Boyer, Tony Kubek, and Pepitone. The only regular to hit over .270 was outfielder Tom Tresh, and he also led the team in home runs with 26. Mantle, now playing left field part of the time instead of center because of his increasingly pain-riddled legs, hit just .255 with 19 home runs. He played in only 122 games.

Sharing a joke before a night game
at Yankee Stadium; from left, Ford,
Collins (15), Berra, Mantle, and Bauer

It was the worst part of his career at that point, and yet he became more appealing to me then than ever before. I think it was his vulnerability that so many fans sensed, still playing a game that was basically finished with him, still mightily struggling to be The Mick when you knew The Mick was gone. Injuries just kept piling up. It seemed incredible that he could play through such pain every day. And the more I learned of his injuries, his ceaseless battles to fight through them and never make excuses for them, the more I loved him. Not simply a reflection of the ultimate competitor, but a man who loved baseball so much that he'd suffer whatever had to be suffered.

In each succeeding season until his retirement at the end of the 1968 season, he came closer and closer to falling below the .300 mark in career average. He was desperate to finish his career above that threshold. He knew the ghost of his father would be livid with him if he dropped below it. But he couldn't give the game up. He was making $100,000 a year and he needed the money because he liked being a generous and big spender and had continued to make bad investments, trusting people who should not have been trusted, the echo of Casey Stengel's quip that he really would have tried to buy the Brooklyn Bridge. But the reasons for continuing to play were far more psychological: the athlete addiction. He knew it and he once described the habit with a simple but beautiful poetry:

"While you're playing ball, all the ballparks and the big crowds have a certain mystique. You feel attached, permanently wedded to the sounds that ring out, to the fans chanting your name, even

Pitching on the warm-up mound at
Yankee Stadium

when there are only four or five thousand fans in the stands on a Wednesday afternoon."

He also began to enjoy the role of senior statesman. He had always had that soft spot in his heart for scared rookies and on-the-fringe players. He knew what it was like to come up to the Yankees feeling as if you didn't belong. In 1966, as the team finished last for the first time in fifty-four years, a rookie named Steve Whitaker joined the club. He idolized Mantle and had no idea what to call him. Mr. Mantle, perhaps? Sir Mantle? His Royal Highness The Mick? It was Mantle who took the initiative and not only introduced himself, but also frequently invited Whitaker over to dinner to keep his chin up. He had done the same thing several years earlier with Tom Tresh when he had come up to the Yankees. Tresh was so indebted to him that he and his wife named their first child Mickey. Instead of being flattered, Mantle seemed more taken aback. Tresh increasingly saw that self-effacement. It led him to conclude that there were two elements missing from an otherwise brilliant repertoire: "knees and confidence."

By 1967 my love affair with Mantle was unrequited.

I was old enough now to go to games at the Stadium with friends. You could walk up to the window on game day and get a ticket, and by the fifth inning you could pretty much sit anywhere and not see anyone else around you for miles. The team drew 1.26 million fans. Given a lineup that included Horace Clarke at second, Ruben Amaro at shortstop, and Charley Smith at third, Mantle was the only reason to go anyway.

From left, Hank Bauer, Mantle,
and Bill Dickey at the batting cage,
spring training, 1953

He was nearing the milestone of his 500th home run. On May 3, 1967, he hit his 499th, against Dave Boswell of the Twins. We all waited for the big one, but Mantle went into a drought. Then I faced a terrible dilemma. My grandfather died in his early nineties. He had led a full and rich life, so the occasion of his passing was not a solemn one. But there was still the matter of the funeral, which took place on May 14. Mickey *still* hadn't hit his 500th, but my father, in one of the greatest paternal moves ever, allowed me to bring a little transistor radio with an earplug. As the eulogies were being given, Mantle did it off Stu Miller at the Stadium. I had the grace not to jump up and scream, but I did whisper to my dad that Mickey had just hit the magic number. My father smiled, then nodded toward the front of the room so at least I would act as if I were listening.

In 1968 Mantle wore the great pinstripes for the last time. At that point everyone thought he should retire. It was wincing to watch him be associated with a team as anemic as the Yankees, even though they did finish four games over .500. Mantle actually led the team in home runs that season with 18, and his 106 walks showed that pitchers either still feared him or knew that behind him in the order was absolutely nobody. On August 22, against the Twins, he hit home run number 534 to tie Jimmie Foxx for third on the all-time list.

He went into a twenty-six-day drought before facing Denny McLain and the Detroit Tigers. The Tigers were on their way to winning the World Series that year. They were feeling magnanimous,

McLain in particular, who won thirty-one games. He was determined to hand Mantle a gimme to break Foxx's record. Mantle looked at the first pitch in the fat zone for a strike and then fouled off the second to go into a 0–2 hole. Exasperated, McLain came off the mound and simply yelled to Mantle to show him where he wanted it. Mantle pointed to the location. McLain spotted it perfectly. Mantle hit home run 535 to move ahead of Foxx. As Madison Square Garden boxing director Harry Markson said, "When a guy has bought 534 drinks in the same saloon, he's entitled to one on the house."

His last home run came off Jim Lonborg of the Boston Red Sox on September 30, hitting from the left side in the third inning before a Stadium crowd of 15,737. Times had changed. The Mets were an inch away from owning New York, led by a pitching staff that included Tom Seaver, Jerry Koosman, and Nolan Ryan. In 1969 the so-called Miracle Mets would win the World Series against the Baltimore Orioles. Earlier that year, in February, during the opening stages of spring training, Mantle went down to Fort Lauderdale. Manager Ralph Houk tried to talk him into another season. The game still tantalized. He also knew he was being used, the Yankees all too aware that they needed Mantle to at least fill some seats. But he said no, pride over need, the acknowledgment that Mickey Mantle the ballplayer had disappeared. When he announced his retirement on March 1 at a press conference, he was, as usual, blunt about what he had become. "I don't hit the ball when I need to. I can't score from second when I need to. I can't steal when I need to."

Hitting a home run left-handed,
Game 4, World Series at Yankee
Stadium, 1956

The summation of his career, as described in a column in the *New York Times* in March 1969, could be encapsulated in the headline alone: "Mantle's Road to Fame: 18 Years of Pain, Misery and Frustration."

"His story must include frustration and unfulfillment along with the glory. Mantle never enjoyed his eighteen years in New York the way many other stars have enjoyed their careers, and injuries and personal struggles were equally responsible."

It was only after his greatness as a player had disappeared that "he was cheered every time he poked his head out of the dugout. However, Mantle understood that the cheers were for him as a descending star and he had never wished to be the central figure in a tragic-opera situation."

Which is exactly what I personified in my Johnny-come-lately love.

From that instant of retirement, Mantle could not find purpose. He could not find peace. Booze became his salve and balm and medication, slowly destroying his liver. It was almost as if you could see, minute by minute, the disintegration of a man who had once seemed immortal in the way that all great athletes seem immortal, until the very second they stop playing and become wanderers, nomads.

My first job, at the *Philadelphia Inquirer* in the early 1980s, was in Atlantic City. Seven casinos had opened by then, but the city was still a pockmarked wreck, the side streets made famous by Monopoly dilapidated single-family homes of narrow two and three stories on shadowy streets. Atlantic Avenue was the commercial skid

row, the northern inlet depopulated like a shipwreck except for the impoverished. It was a seedy place to work regardless of the high rollers and the casino moguls promising greatness to come.

The Claridge was the most modest of the hotel-casinos. It was small. It had been refurbished quickly to take advantage of the gambling legislation. In its attempt at sophistication, the door-men dressed in British beefeater uniforms in the tradition of the real Claridge's, in London. It was comical, particularly when the South Jersey and Philadelphia accents came out and the doormen tended to say, "Yo! Welcome to Claridge's!"

Ford, Berra, Martin, Maris, Mantle,
and DiMaggio at Old-Timers' Day,
Yankee Stadium, 1978

Like many, I had lost track of Mickey Mantle. It wasn't that he entirely faded away, because he never faded away, but I had heard virtually nothing of him since his retirement. I knew that he was carted out every now and then for a Mickey Mantle Day or Old-Timers' game at the Stadium, but I also knew it was a transparent attempt to create some excitement for fans, the great Mick coming back home.

When it was announced that Mantle had become director of sports promotions for the Claridge, my heart sank. From working in Atlantic City, I knew what that meant—he was willing to sell himself for $100,000 a year by acting as a sop to high rollers who had as much class as the gaudy gold they fancied, rings as big as fists, chains nearing their navels that made bling look blank. It was degrading, and I think Mantle knew it was degrading. I later learned that he was drinking more heavily than ever then, and his self-degradation was now accompanied by acrid bitterness and even more balm of the booze.

During the eighties he engaged in what Jane Leavy called "performance art," polishing up stories to give reporters exactly what they wanted, the fatalistic ex-ballplayer excommunicated from the game he loved because of the great athletic evil of time when the body and timing and bat speed no longer worked as they once did. He told a female reporter about a dream he kept having in which he couldn't get into Yankee Stadium and nobody knew who he was. The anecdote turned out to be untrue, and yet it was true.

Laughing at Yankee Stadium, 1956

He was so desperately lost. He also railed at the icon image more than ever. In 1973, when the Yankees were preparing a celebration of the fiftieth anniversary of the opening of the House That Ruth Built, a questionnaire was sent to players. Mantle's answers were angry, dismissive, at total odds with all he had done. He signed his name at the end and then added at the bottom "The All-American Boy." He meant it as a mockery of himself and the label.

Looking for ways to make money, because he was always looking for ways to make money, he matched up with Whitey Ford at harness tracks to ride the ponies and toured with clown prince

Signing baseballs before a game in
the Yankee Stadium locker room,
1955

Max Patkin. Mantle made himself a willing fool, an on-the-road spectacle, a dancing bear.

He was grasping, until the card memorabilia industry exploded and Mantle became its most lucrative recipient. Typically, he insisted that old teammates attend card shows with him so they could get some piece of the action. But once again he felt like a sellout. He signed balls with profanities and crude phrases, but they still sold for as much as $6,700. Fans still loved him. He still meant so much to them. Yet he too often did his best to alienate them.

Billy Martin died in 1989, killed in a car crash after drinking. There will always be debate as to whether Martin was the instigator of Mantle's copious drinking with the Yankees or just a partner to it. Nobody back in Commerce liked Martin very much, particularly when, fresh off a divorce, he came to live with Mickey and Merlyn for the summer and basically turned every day into one drinking binge after another with his teammate. Mantle himself said that Martin never forced him to drink. He was a pallbearer at his funeral, and his death left him more isolated than ever.

The drinking only escalated. Clete Boyer said that the only way Mantle could get to sleep at night was by drinking and the only way he could get up in the morning was by drinking. But there seemed more at play. It seemed as if he was using the booze not simply to anesthetize himself but also to kill himself.

Until he realized he *was* killing himself, willfully or not.

In 1994, on the eve of entering the Betty Ford Clinic for his alcoholism, perhaps the most important decision of his life other

FOLLOWING: Playing with a toy ball on a string with Billy Martin in the Yankee Stadium locker room, 1955

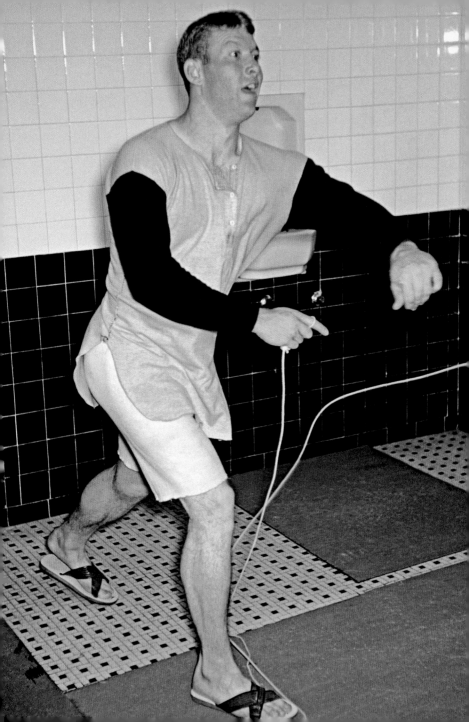

than not going back home to the mines of Oklahoma when the Yankees had sent him down to Kansas City in the middle of his rookie season in 1951, Mantle did an exclusive interview with Bob Costas on NBC.

I have seen many interviews of celebrities, which of course Mantle was and always would be. But I have never seen one such as this, so sincere, so honest without a hint of posturing, in which he talked about his failures—the liquor, the pervasive sense that he was not a good man and never lived up to what he could have been as a player, the unforgivable neglect of his four sons and Merlyn,

Mantle and Billy Martin at
Old-Timers' Day, Yankee Stadium,
1978

all of whom ultimately went into treatment for drug dependencies. Like father, like son. Like husband, like wife. His sons loved him or at least tried to love him. But they barely knew him, a figurehead who popped into the home in Dallas every now and then and then popped out. Danny and Mickey Jr. were deep into cheap wine at thirteen. Billy and David advanced further, into cocaine. They were all lost without him. And deep inside he was lost without them, but never an emotional man—men whose origins are in the mines don't have time for emotion because the land takes all they have—he could not show it.

Mantle had been interviewed on television thousands of times at that point. He knew the game, his ability to throw enough hilarious one-liners to maintain his folksy aura. But his appearance with Costas wasn't an interview at all. It was an intimate and confessional conversation between two friends in which one was finally telling the other all that had been inside him for so many years. The tone in Mantle's voice was a constant of soft sorrow. His blue eyes were mellow with shame. He slumped in his chair. There was no drama or primping in front of the camera the way celebrities do even when describing their downfall. He didn't care about that. The words came out of him without censorship; he refused to hold back on anything. When he cried, there was no sense of "cue the tears." There was no payoff—a tell-all book in the works, a circuit of television appearances culminating on *Oprah* (it was the only television interview he did before entering the clinic; Jill Lieber also interviewed him, for a piece in *Sports Illustrated*). It was just that Oklahoma twang, needing to give explanation for his increasingly self-destructive behavior that anyone going to his restaurant on Central Park South in New York, Mickey Mantle's, could see when he was drinking, just as they could see the great glimpses of charm and warmth when he wasn't drinking or at least could hold his liquor.

Courage, like too many other words of its type in the English language, has become overused. It has no meaning anymore. Maybe I am making the same mistake. But I saw such courage in Mantle in that interview. I saw a man, still a hero to millions, say things about himself that I have never heard anyone in the public eye ever admit. I also saw a man, that face so sagging, not a single remnant of the gorgeous Yankee he had once been, so utterly broken, as if a strain of incurable virus were coursing through his veins without hope of a cure except for this one final chance, at Betty Ford. Never had I seen anyone so human. Never in my life have I admired a public figure as much as I admired Mantle after that interview.

I was fortunate enough to watch a tape of the interview with Costas. We were working on a book together, and his feelings about Mantle only gave me more insight. "He was acutely aware of his shortcomings and they weighed on him heavily. Most significantly as a husband and father. Even as a ballplayer he felt that despite the injuries and congenital conditions that compromised

Close-up portrait at Yankee
Stadium, 1957

him . . . if he had taken better care of himself he could have gotten more out of his ability.

"He was painfully aware of the gap between who he wanted to be and in some sense could have been and [who] he most often was."

Costas had grown up as a devout Yankee fan, and Mantle had played an enormous role in that devotion. Costas loved Mantle in the way that so many kids loved him, or Willie Mays, or Hank Aaron, all of whom represented the epitome of baseball in the 1950s and early 1960s, when it was still the national pastime yet cloaked in a certain kind of innocence without megaton deals and free agency signings. Players played because they wanted to play. While they cared about how much they got paid, they would have played anyway.

Costas had met Mantle at various points after his career was long behind him, the first occasion when Mantle was inducted into the Hall of Fame in 1974. He got to know him particularly well when they both spent long stretches at the Regency Hotel, Bob because of work at NBC's headquarters in Rockefeller Center, Mantle because of the restaurant that opened in 1988 and is still there on Central Park South. Bob had still loved Mantle, but his feelings about him were not through colored glasses shielding the glare of the truth. He saw Mantle's strengths, the good qualities that were still within him when he allowed himself to reveal them.

One night they went to the Post House in New York to have dinner. Mantle ate some of his steak and then asked the waiter to wrap up the rest. It struck Costas as an odd request, since Mantle could order room service whenever he wanted. It was a cold New York

Shaving in the Yankee Stadium
locker room, 1955

night, but Mantle insisted on taking a circuitous route and stopped in front of a cardboard box and knocked on it. The head of a homeless man popped out. "Hi, Mick," he said, making it clear that they knew each other. Mantle then handed him the doggie bag of food, an act that Mantle repeated as much as he could.

One night Mantle went to Costas's house in St. Louis for dinner. Cardinal Hall of Famer Stan Musial was there. Mickey had not entered the Betty Ford Clinic yet, and out of deference to Musial, he had maybe one drink. It was one of those wonderful evenings of baseball storytelling between two baseball immortals. After Musial left, Mantle remarked on what a great person Musial was, but Mantle believed he was the one with more natural ability. "Stan had a better career than me because he's a better man than me," he told Costas that night. The shivering acknowledgment of that couldn't help but permeate the toughest bones of the most suspicious and cynical, except for the few who would always propagate Mantle's lost potential.

But Costas also saw the dark side, so off-putting, so boorish and unbearable when stoked by drink, the infamous breakfast of champions that he liked to brag about: Kahlúa, brandy, and cream. He witnessed an occasion at the restaurant where a youngster came up to Mantle to ask for an autograph. Mickey had retreated to a back booth, and the child was warned that Mantle did not like to sign autographs. But Mantle was his idol. He went ahead anyway and asked him if he in fact did like to sign autographs. "No!" bellowed Mantle in a way that was mean and hurtful, so unnecessary.

Mantle as a pitcher, taking the catcher's signal

PREVIOUS: DiMaggio, Mantle, Maris, Martin, Berra, and Ford at Old-Timers' Day, Yankee Stadium, 1978

Costas was at an event for the Children's Miracle Network in 1993 in Oklahoma. Musial was there and Moose Skowron and Hank Bauer and former Red Sox pitcher Dick Radatz. So was Mantle, who became so drunk that Saturday night that he told a woman in front of her husband that he had always wanted to sleep with her. The next morning at the buffet line, he was still ripped.

"It was heartbreaking," said Costas. "And I remember saying to myself, 'I can't come to this stuff anymore. I can't be here anymore.' It got to the point that when the haze of alcohol was around him, you wondered if anything was registering."

A young fan photographing Mantle
at spring training, Florida, 1953

For much of 1993, depression was a part of his life. He did think about killing himself.

In December, as Mantle himself tells it, he went to a charity golf tournament in Atlanta. A dinner followed, and Mantle was cursing and crude. He knew his behavior had been inexcusable.

He spoke to Pat Summerall, the former New York Giants kicker and CBS football broadcaster who had had his own difficult bout of alcoholism and had gone to the Betty Ford Clinic. Mantle had his liver examined by a doctor, who told him that the organ, because of his drinking, had healed itself so many times it was soon going to look like one big scab. "The next drink you take might be your last," the doctor said.

Nobody really knew if Mantle would actually get on the plane to Palm Springs to go to the center in February 1994. Mantle himself didn't really know if he could go through with it. But he did because much like playing with injury, he always persevered when committed to something. He was there for thirty-two days. His room number was 202. At first it was impossible for him to talk about his family without crying. As part of the program he wrote a letter to his father, Mutt. He cried the whole time. He said that he loved him and wished he could have told him that when he was alive. He also wrote that he wished Mutt could have been alive to see him after his rookie season, when he did have so many seasons and moments of magnificence.

He had to keep a journal. He took it home with him after those thirty-two days. It wasn't very long, but scribbled in the margins

FOLLOWING: Billy Hunter, Don Larsen, and Mantle relaxing after a game in the locker room, 1955

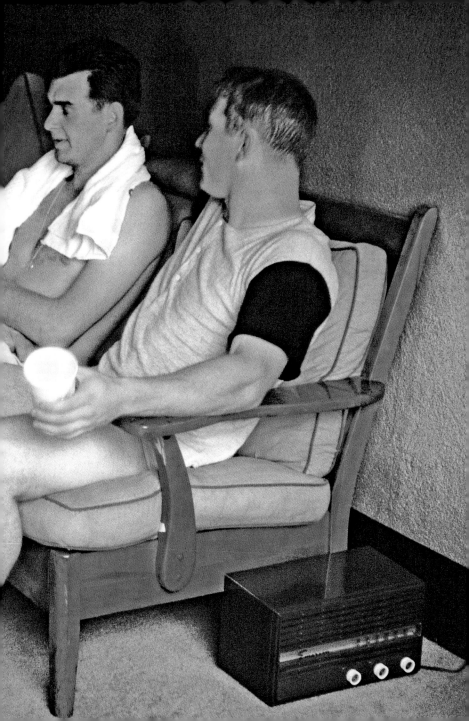

were the words "embarrassed," "angry," "humiliated," "foolish," "ashamed," "stupid," "guilty," "inadequate," and "exasperated."

"In the dictionary of self-loathing, I don't think I missed much," Mantle said in a book he later wrote, but the very expression was cathartic. "It helped me face my faults and my mistakes. I felt different and I was determined to stay sober."

The weight of tragedy that always rode on Mantle's shoulders did not take long to be supremely tested after he left Betty Ford. In March 1994, his son Billy died of a heart attack at thirty-six. Since his diagnosis of Hodgkin's as a teenager, an experimental chemotherapy treatment had kept him up screaming at night, followed by his getting hooked on drugs and alcohol, followed by heart bypass surgery. He was the same age as his father had been when he'd last played for the Yankees, but there was no special day at Yankee Stadium to commemorate the occasion. According to Leavy, he died in a correctional treatment center after having been arrested for driving under the influence.

Mantle was playing golf at Preston Trail Golf Club in Dallas when he received the news. Guilt naturally flooded him, the impact that his own drinking had had upon his son, the lack of presence as a father. As Mickey told it, he felt himself tempted to have a drink at the club, just a glass of wine maybe. He knew it could never be just one, because it was never just one.

He left the club.

Mickey Mantle changed with the same honesty and sincerity that had always marked his life. But it was in a positive way now,

With Casey Stengel in a dugout
portrait at Yankee Stadium, 1956

with the same full-bore commitment. He became close to his three remaining boys, Mickey Jr., David, and Danny. Although he and Merlyn were separated, they were still married, and their support for each other was unparalleled.

The weight of tragedy left him alone for a while. He became the man he had always wanted to be but had so mightily resisted, or at least as close to that man as he possibly could be. He was given a respite from the demons, maybe even a final parting. But the curse was always there, his life always an unpredictable earthquake.

On May 28, 1995, he entered the Baylor University Medical Center after the diagnosis that he had cancer of the liver. He needed a transplant, and all the controversy over whether he jumped to the top of the list over more deserving candidates was wrong: Without it he would have died in just days, a crucial criterion. He received the liver transplant, but as they were doing the surgery they discovered that the cancer had spread into his pancreas. Had the surgeons discovered it ahead of time, Mantle would have been deemed too sick for a transplant and another patient would have received one. But there was no way of knowing except by doing the surgery.

At the time in his life when Mickey Mantle finally knew what he wanted, what he wanted to be as a father and what he wanted to be for his fans, there was no time. There was something so fatalistic in that. But also something painfully fitting, because Mantle's timing, except in baseball, had never been very good.

He rapidly lost weight. He subsisted on protein drinks

At the Pittsburgh World Series,
Heinz Field, 1960

because eating solids was impossible. He was gaunt and ghostly, a feather. He held his last press conference on July 11. He was funny as usual, asking one of the collectors who had helped to corner the Mickey Mantle memorabilia market, "Did you get my other liver?" But then he turned serious. He was trying to leave the legacy he felt was most important:

"I'd like to say to kids out there, if you're looking for a role model, this is a role model. Don't be like me." It was such a powerful statement, but as usual he was too hard on himself. In the final year of his life he had proved that a man could look at himself in the mirror and legitimately change; see all the crisscrosses of cracks and instead of just accepting them, vow at least to make amends for them. Before he finished, Mantle had one more thing to say, the wounds of self-loathing and regret never able to heal, never ever fully comfortable with himself:

"God gave me a body and an ability to play baseball. God gave me everything and I just . . ."

He didn't finish the sentence.

The cancer spread like brushfire—speeding uncontrollably into his new liver, his lungs, the lining of his heart. He knew death could come at any moment now, any second. Never one for religion, he asked a friend if he could arrange a baptism. Never at a loss for mordant humor, he appeared on the JumboTron of Yankee Stadium on July 22, 1995, in honor of the hundredth anniversary of Babe Ruth's birth, and said, "I feel like Phil Rizzuto in Babe Ruth's uniform."

Behind the batting cage, St.
Petersburg, Florida, 1953

He entered the hospital for good on July 28. He restricted his visitors but he embraced his teammates, clinging to the memories of when he had been the safest and most happy in life, as close as he could get now to that eternal boy's game. Hank Bauer came to the hospital. So did Johnny Blanchard and Moose Skowron and Whitey Ford.

Several minutes after midnight on August 13, 1995, he briefly awoke and took the hands of Merlyn and his son David. Forty minutes later he was dead.

His funeral took place two days later at the Lovers Lane United Methodist Church in Dallas. The church overflowed. Bobby Richardson, a man of deep religious conviction and about as opposite from the lifestyle of Mantle as one could get, officiated because they had always loved each other. Former teammates came from everywhere, with the notable exception of Joe DiMaggio, petulant to the end. At Mantle's request, Costas gave the eulogy, not simply because they were friends, but because Mantle felt he captured the meaning of baseball better than anyone else. On that day, in just a few sentences, Costas also captured the meaning of Mantle better than anyone else:

He was our symbol of baseball at a time when the game meant something to us that perhaps it no longer does. Mickey Mantle had those dual qualities so seldom seen, exuding dynamism and excitement, but at the same time touching your heart— flawed, wounded. We knew there was something poignant

Mantle leaving the dugout to bat with Hank Bauer seated to his left, Fenway Park, 1956

about Mickey Mantle before we knew what poignant meant.
We didn't just root for him. We felt for him.

Country singer Roy Clark, also at Mantle's request, sang the song "Yesterday When I Was Young."

It was a sentimental song so typical of Mantle's sentimentality, the man who cried at *The Last Picture Show* because he knew so well what it was like to live in a place where there were no breaks in life, only what you made of it and the luck you needed to make it.

When I began to read biographies of Mantle to write this book, it was impossible not to notice how many used the word "hero" in their titles. Given the failures in his life, I wondered if that was truly an accurate way of describing him or simply a romantic one.

I was wrong.

He was a hero, a complex hero, a human hero with the contradiction and conflict and complication that exists in all of us, which only makes him more heroic and everlasting.

There were better players in his own era. There are better players now. There will be better players in the future. It is the nature of sports, the great gifts of an athlete always replaced by the greater gifts of another. His statistics still stand tall. But they tell so little.

There will never be another like him. Never.

Smiling near the batting cage, Old-Timers' Day, Yankee Stadium, 1978

A Note on Sources

In writing on Mickey Mantle I used a variety of different sources. First and foremost was Jane Leavy's exceptional biography of Mantle, *The Last Boy*. David Faulkner's *The Last Hero*, the memoir *A Hero All His Life* by the Mantle family, Tony Castro's *Mickey Mantle*, Marty Appel's *Now Pitching for the Yankees*, and Jim Bouton's *Ball Four* were also very helpful. I relied heavily on coverage of Mantle in the *New York Times* during his career. My magazine sources included *Sports Illustrated*, *Time*, and *Popular Science*. In writing about specific games, I went dozens of times to the marvelous Web site Retrosheet.org, which has compiled box scores and inning-by-inning recaps of virtually ever major league baseball game ever played. I also combed through dozens of Web sites dedicated to Mantle. Finally, I am indebted to Bob Costas for both his time and his keen and eloquent insights.

Locker room at the spring training facility, St. Petersburg, Florida

PREVIOUS: Hitting a home run left-handed, Game 4, World Series, Yankee Stadium, 1956

Acknowledgments

It is the state of the technological world of today that you never meet the people you work with face-to-face to make a book such as this one come to life. It is unfortunate, because *The Classic Mantle* never would have been realized without the hard labor of the good people at Abrams. A hearty thank-you goes out to editorial director of the Adult trade division Jennifer Levesque, associate managing editor Jen Graham, assistant editor Wesley Royce, production manager Tina Cameron, and designer Kara Strubel. I hope one day to see if all of you actually exist. I offer gratitude as usual to the saintly Lisa for putting up with me. I would also be remiss not to mention the contribution of my most loyal friend, the wonder yellow Lab Maddy. Finally, there is Mickey Mantle. I never met him; I sorely wish I had. But he will always have a prominent place in my heart.

—*Buzz Bissinger*

To Mickey Mantle, whose friendship still lives in my photographs. To Abrams' publisher, Steve Tager, for making the book happen. To my editor, Jennifer Levesque, and art director, Kara Strubel, for their dedicated professionalism. To my wife, Brigitte, for her support and patience. To Al Silverman, my dear friend who shares all the Mantle memories with me. To Christopher Sweet, for his ongoing advice and help.

—*Marvin E. Newman*

About the Author

BUZZ BISSINGER is the author of five books, including the *New York Times* bestsellers *Three Nights in August* and *Friday Night Lights*, which has sold close to two million copies and spawned a film and television show. His most recent book, *Father's Day*, is about his relationship with his disabled son, Zachary. He is a contributing editor for *Vanity Fair* and a sports columnist for the *Daily Beast*. He has written for *Sports Illustrated*, the *New York Times*, *GQ*, the *New Republic*, *Newsweek*, and *Time*.

About the Photographer

MARVIN E. NEWMAN is the photographer of *Yankee Colors: The Glory Years of the Mantle Era*. He has been a national president of the American Society of Media Photographers and a contributing photographer to *Sports Illustrated*. His work has been exhibited at museums across the country, including the Museum of Modern Art and the Metropolitan Museum of Art in New York and the Art Institute in Chicago. He is represented by the Bruce Silverstein Gallery in New York and the Stephen Daiter Gallery in Chicago.

Published in 2012 by Stewart, Tabori & Chang
An imprint of ABRAMS

Library of Congress Cataloging-in-Publication Data

Bissinger, H. G.
  The classic Mantle / Buzz Bissinger ; photographs by Marvin E. Newman.
    p. cm.
  ISBN 978-1-58479-986-3 (alk. paper)
1. Mantle, Mickey, 1931–1995. 2. Baseball players—United States—Biography. 3. New York Yankees
(Baseball team)—History. I. Title.
  GV865.M33B57 2012
  796.357092—dc23
  [B]
                    2012016789

EDITOR: Jennifer Levesque
SERIES DESIGN: Galen Smith
PRODUCTION MANAGER: Tina Cameron

The text of this book was composed in Fliosofia and Trade Gothic.

Printed and bound in U.S.A.
10 9 8 7 6 5 4 3 2 1

Stewart, Tabori & Chang books are available at special discounts when purchased
in quantity for premiums and promotions as well as fundraising or educational
use. Special editions can also be created to specification. For details, contact
specialsales@abramsbooks.com or the address below.

THE ART OF BOOKS SINCE 1949

115 West 18th Street
New York, NY 10011
www.abramsbooks.com